THE INSTANT GENIUS

THE INSTANT GENIUS

An Indispensable Handbook
for Know-It-Alls

by

Tanya Slover

General Publishing Group
Los Angeles

Publisher: W. Quay Hays
Editorial Director: Peter L. Hoffman
Editor: Steve Baeck
Art Director and Cover Design: Maritta Tapanainen
Production Director: Trudihope Schlomowitz
Prepress Manager: Bill Castillo

For information:
General Publishing Group, Inc.
2701 Ocean Park Boulevard, Suite 140
Santa Monica, CA 90405

Library of Congress Cataloging-in-Publication Data

Slover, Tanya.
    The instant genius : an indispensable handbook for know-it-
alls / by Tanya Slover.
    p.   cm.
    ISBN 1-57544-099-7 (pbk.)
    1. Questions and answers. I. Title.
AG195.S554 1998   98-35454
031'.02—dc21   CIP

Printed in the USA by RR Donnelley & Sons Company

10 9 8 7 6 5 4 3 2 1

General Publishing Group
Los Angeles

FOREWORD

A lot of what you'll read in *The Instant Genius* has been rattling around in my head for years. "Why don't you write this stuff down?" a friend said to me one day over lunch. "Who knows? Maybe somebody else will think it's interesting, too?"

I decided to give it a try. But I didn't know how I would tell others about all that "stuff" in my head and make it worth the read. Many of the trivia books I had skimmed were only a sketchy recital of marginally interesting information. I mean, how many people care who won the World Series in 1952 or what the name of the last passenger pigeon was to become extinct?*

After opting for a question-and-answer format, I contacted various museums and libraries, called title companies, checked out the Internet, and reviewed an assortment of encyclopedias to refresh my memory about what I thought I knew. I also made telephone calls to experts in many different fields and discovered even they were curious about the book I proposed writing. After all, how often do you telephone a perfect stranger (in this case an entomologist), and start the conversation off asking him to describe the sexual parts of a flea's anatomy?

Although I've researched and verified the information in this book to the best of my ability, *The Instant Genius* is obviously tongue-in-cheek and not meant to be scholarly, but simply entertaining—an enjoyable way to pick up interesting facts and tidbits to share with others.

*In case you do, it was the Yankees in 1952 and Martha in 1914.

ACKNOWLEDGMENTS

A sincere thanks to Judith Andrews for suggesting that I write a book about all "that stuff" rattling around in my head.

And a very special thanks to Jeanette Longlad for her help and enthusiasm in shaping this book. I sometimes think just as much "stuff" is rattling around in her head.

What famous Renaissance painter, inventor, and sculptor briefly sculpted in "marzipan" (a confection of almond paste, egg whites, and sugar) for his patron, Prince Ludovico Sforza of Milan?

Leonardo da Vinci (1452–1519). However, he was not amused when the prince and his court devoured his work. According to an article by Tor Eigeland in *Aramco World*, Leonardo groused in his *Notes on Cuisine*: "I have observed with pain that my signor Ludovico and his court gobble up all the sculptures I give them, right to the last morsel, and now I am determined to find other means that do not taste as good, so that my works may survive."

What internationally renowned gourmet chef was a spy for the Allies during World War II?

Julia Child. Julia's culinary talents developed later, after the war ended and after a stint at Paris's Cordon Bleu.

What short story, written by Morgan Robertson in 1898, eerily mirrors many details about the Titanic's maiden voyage 14 years later in 1912?

"The Wreck of the Titan," in a book by the same name*, tells about a fabulous, "unsinkable" ocean liner that struck an iceberg in the Atlantic one cold April evening (just like the Titanic). Named the Titan, this fictional ship was far larger than any that had ever been built and lavishly appointed to carry the rich and famous. The passenger capacity in both the fictitious Titan and the actual Titanic was about 3,000 people and both ships had only enough lifeboats for about half that. Apart from these staggering similarities, it seems that the length of both ships, their tons displacement, their speed, and their triple-screw propulsion were close approximations of each other.

*The full title of Morgan Robertson's book is "The Wreck of the Titan or Futility."

What famous person was said to have uttered the following words in his death bed: "This wallpaper is killing me. One of us has to go"?

Poet and playwright Oscar Wilde.

How did the expression, "mad as a hatter," supposedly originate?

To describe some of the hatters and tailors of centuries past who worked with mercury. Mercury is toxic to the nervous systerm, so many of them invariably went bonkers.

What piece of sports equipment has been used to raise a sunken ship?

Ping-Pong balls. Hundreds of thousands of them were used to displace the water in the hull of a sunken ship blocking a Scandanavian harbor entrance. Once the hull was full, the ship rose right up out of the water.

What handsome Victorian adventurer disguised himself as an Afghan Muslim and made the pilgrimage to Mecca?

Captain Sir Richard Francis Burton. Other than being a famous explorer who once searched for the source of the Nile, Burton was also a great intellect, scholar, soldier, scientist, and undercover agent. He spoke over two dozen languages, including many dialects, wrote numerous books, and translated several classic works of erotica into English, including *The Kama Sutra, The Perfumed Garden,* and *Arabian Nights.* NOTE: Infidels, or non-Muslims, were not allowed to visit Mecca. Had Burton been discovered he would have undoubtedly been killed.

What ancient book suggested positions like "Exposed Gills, Unicorn's Horn and Firm Attachment" for lovemaking?

Ars Amatoria, the famous Chinese love book, by Master Tung-Hsuan.

What is one of the most graphic textbooks on sex and love ever written?

The Kama Sutra of Vatsyayana, subtitled *The Hindu Art of Love.*

What was first book printed in this country (while it was still made up of colonies)?

The Bay Psalm Book or, as it is known by its full title, *The Whole Booke of Psalms Faithfully Translated Into English Metre.* Few of the 1,700 copies printed in 1640 have survived, making it one of the most valuable books in the English language.

What color are the beautiful, white Lippizaner horses when they are born?

Black, sometimes gray.

What plane, built in the 1960s, flew from coast to coast in less than 70 minutes on March 6, 1990?

The Blackbird (SR-71), a spy plane. The flight from Palmdale, California, to Washington, D.C., lasted 68 minutes and 17 seconds. For decades, SR-71 was the fastest bird around and may still be the fastest. Its top speed has never been declassified. Though the Blackbird has been officially replaced by satellites and the TR-I, several SR-71s were recently recommissioned.

How do honey bees communicate?

They dance. Specifically, the worker bees (all female) do a "waggle dance" to tell the others the direction and distance to the nectar.

Why doesn't Hindi, the official language of India, have a word for lesbian?

It's anyone's guess.

Why were paste-on "beauty marks" worn in 17th-century Europe?

To cover up smallpox scars. Owing to several devastating epidemics, more than half the population of Europe had facial scars.

What was one of the biggest killer epidemics of all time?

The flu pandemic (worldwide epidemic) of 1918, also known as Spanish influenza. Considering that it lasted less than a year and killed over 22 million worldwide (some sources say up to 40 million), it beats even the bubonic plague in lethality. The bubonic plague killed more people but lasted a lot longer. Where the 1918 flu came from and where it went no one knows. Will it ever show up again? The experts don't know that either.

What famous piece of real estate other than Pompeii did that famous circus master, P. T. Barnum, purportedly once try to buy?

Niagara Falls.

Who was the first person to go over Niagara Falls in a barrel?

A woman named Anna Edson Taylor. When the coroner tried to stop her, a defiant Anna threatened to jump over the Falls and leave a real mess to clean up. He relented and Anna barreled her way into history on October 24, 1901.

Can you name at least one English word that has no rhyming partner? Hint: There are only four of them and three of them are colors. Second hint: One of the colors is a fruit and one is a metal.

Purple, orange, silver, and month.

How old is a saguaro cactus before it starts growing its first arm?

Between 60 and 80 years old. It takes a long time to become a full-fledged saguaro.

What newly emerging scientific discipline uses bugs and insects to tell police when people died?

Forensic entomology. Different insects invade a corpse at different times depending on temperature, weather, location of the body (outside or inside), etc., providing evidence as to when a person died.

Dr. William Moulton Marston, the inventor of the lie detector, created what crime-fighting cartoon character?

Wonder Woman.

Leonardo da Vinci's "airscrew" was a precursor of what 20th-century invention?

The helicopter.

What was the first ship in history to send out an SOS?

The Titanic. Shortly before the night it sank in April 1912, an international convention agreed to replace "CQD" ("Come Quickly, Distress"), the traditional call for help, with "SOS" ("Save Our Souls"). The latter distress call was considered easier to recognize. The Titanic used both that fateful night.

What is a draggletail?

A whore in days of yore.

What is the etymology, or word derivation, of *pornography*?

From the Greek, *pornographos* (*porne* = prostitute + *graphein* = to write), *Webster's New World Dictionary* gives its original meaning as "writing about prostitutes."

In antiquity, where did prostitutes ply their trade?

In temples throughout Greece and Rome. At the time, prostitution was considered sacred, and sex a holy rite. Money earned was used to maintain the temple and provide for the "sacred women" who lived there.

What well-known movie critic wrote the screenplay for the 1970 movie *Beyond the Valley of the Dolls*?

Roger Ebert.

What representative democracy supposedly served as one of the models for the American system?

The Iroquois Nation.* This Confederacy of six Indian tribes, or nations, practiced democracy in its purest form. It is said that Benjamin Franklin and Thomas Jefferson were influenced by many of its ideas. A couple of the things the Founding Fathers borrowed were the impeachment of leaders and the caucus. A cornerstone of our whole democratic system, the caucus is a meeting of the leaders of a political party to formulate policy and/or pick candidates to lead them. The newly born United States, however, departed from the Iroquois Nation in several crucial respects. It did not treat women or others as equals.

* Benjamin Franklin is said to have acknowledged the impact of the Iroquois political system when drafting the U.S. Constitution. Many scholars, however, refute this.

Why doesn't an elevator stop at the 13th floor?

Owing to superstition, most buildings don't designate a 13th floor. The nomenclature simply jumps from the 12th to the 14th.

13

Who painted postcards for sale to tourists before becoming one of the most ignominious dictators in history?

Adolf Hitler. He liked doing watercolor scenes.

Did Hitler ever own land in the United States?

It depends on whom you talk to and what you read. According to several accounts, Hitler inherited nearly 9,000 acres of land in 1942 near the small town of Kit Carson (about 150 miles east of Denver) from relatives living in Germany. But the locals of Kit Carson say they don't know whether the tale about the "Hitler Land" is true or not. The town clerk says she's heard the story for as long she can remember but hasn't been able to verify it. The Cheyenne County Astract Company, a title company in the area, says they have no record of Hitler owning land. However, they point out that in the early 1940s the acreage in question was seized by the U.S. government under the Alien Act, as were all holdings of citizens of enemy nations. At the time a person with a German surname held title. Was it a straw person for the Furor's real estate aspirations in Colorado? Unlikely. However, if the story were true, would Hitler have put his name on the title? Not likely.

What high-ranking Nazi leader was once a chicken farmer?

Heinrich Himmler, commander of the SS and Gestapo. At one time he was also a salesman for a fertilizer company.

What famous actress portrayed the character of Hamlet in the first movie version?

Sarah Bernhardt. In 1900, she did a movie short in which she played Hamlet in the duel scene.

What human being made a successful career out of farting?

A Frenchman named Joseph Pujol had remarkable gas-passing skills. His repertoire included playing the scales and imitating a little girl in springtime, tooting air as she merrily skipped along. "Le Petomane (The Farter or Fartiste)," as Pujol was called, became so popular he reportedly once outdrew Sarah Bernhardt, who was appearing in Paris at the same time.

What celebrated showman offered a large sum of money for Sarah Bernhardt's amputated leg?

P. T. Barnum in 1915. He wanted the rights to exhibit her severed limb.

What kid-hating misanthrope said, "My heart is a bargain today. Will you take it?"

W. C. Fields.

What famous general, renowned for his military genius, was a homosexual who took his lover with him on many of his campaigns?

Alexander the Great.

What is spontaneous human combustion?

The sudden, unexplained ignition of a human body into flames resulting in its almost instantaneous, fiery demise. In one case, all that remained of the victim was the woman's shoed foot and a pile of ashes. The surrounding area was untouched by fire. The phenomenon is dismissed by most scientists as pure poppycock.

What famous English king exploded in his casket and sent the funeral congregation fleeing from the church?

William the Conqueror, king of England from 1066 to 1087. Poor William suffered internal injuries when he fell from his horse on the way to a health spa to lose weight. After languishing several days in beastly hot and humid weather, he finally succumbed. Too fat for his sarcophagus (stone coffin), the monks were forced to force his ample body inside. The pressure of his festering innards proved too much and William simply exploded from all the pent-up pus.

Who were a couple of English kings that didn't speak English?

William the Conqueror (1066–1087) was Norman, or French; George I (1714–1727) was a German.

What very intelligent, hale, and hearty queen of England outlived both her husbands and 8 of her 10 children?

Eleanor of Aquitaine, immortalized on screen by Katharine Hepburn in *The Lion in Winter*. Eleanor was the wife of Louis VII of France and Henry II of England. She was also the mother of two very famous children: Richard the Lionhearted; and King John, who signed the Magna Carta (although under duress), a forerunner of our Bill of Rights. She died in 1204 at the age of 82.

What famous English 17th-century revolutionary leader was beheaded two years after he died?

Oliver Cromwell (1599–1658), Lord Protector of the Commonwealth. Charles II had the Lord Protector's body exhumed, publicly hanged, and then decapitated in revenge for Cromwell's beheading of his father, Charles I, nine years before.

What queen of England had an extra finger on one hand as well as a supernumerary, or extra, nipple?

Anne Boleyn, the second wife of Henry VIII, mother of Queen Elizabeth I.

What English monarch is credited with inventing the closet?

Elizabeth I. Needing somewhere to stash all her dresses (in the thousands), she had a special room designed with a hanger, or hook, for each and every dress.

What strange disease might possibly explain King George III's (r.1760–1820) madness? Note: He was the King of England when the American colonies won their independence from England.

Porphyia, a disease that causes a rare metabolic disturbance, could be the culprit. The condition creates a pigment imbalance in the blood that poisons the nervous system and discolors the urine, turning it a burgundy wine or a black color (some say blue).

Who was one of Sir Winston Churchill's frequent dining partners?

His cat, Jock. The pussy ate right at the table with him.

Who made the following, unfortunate observation: "I learned the way a monkey learns—by watching its parents"?

Prince Charles.

Who colonized Australia?

Convicts. England originally set it up as a penal colony.

If a person is an expert at prestidigitation, what's the art at which he or she excels?

Sleight of hand. Magic. Trickery.

And the legerdemain expert?

The same.

What is *Teufelbuhlschaft* or "devil's love"?

Sexual attraction to and copulation with the devil. Such a concept figured in Church literature for centuries as one of the "sins of complete lechery."

What, other than the devil theory, might explain the Salem witchcraft hysteria?

A common fungus. Ergot, a parasitic fungus growing on rye and other grains, can cause ergot poisoning. Symptoms include dilated pupils, anaesthesia, tingling, twitching in the extremities, and, occasionally, convulsions. As if this weren't enough, ergot is the source of a powerful hallucinogen, lysergic acid diethylamide (LSD). No wonder those girls thought they were consorting with the devil.

What was the *Malleus Maleficarum,* or *Witches' Hammer?*

The official witch-hunting manual used in Europe for three centuries. Published circa 1486 by two Dominican monks, James Sprenger and Heinrich Kramer, the book was an instant success and christened the indisputable authority for tracking down, trying and killing witches.

What item commonly found in every American household was used to perform frontal lobotomies in the '40s and '50s?

An ice pick. American neurologist Walter Freeman performed thousands of transorbital lobotomies with an ice pick he kept in his pocket. His last "operation" was in 1967.

What 1920s world-famous dancer accidentally strangled herself?

Isadora Duncan. While riding in a roadster, the long scarf around her neck became entangled in the spokes of one of the car's wheels and choked her to death.

What macho sportsman and writer loved cats?

Ernest Hemingway. He left a trust to care for all the kitties who kept him company on Key West and for their offspring.

What makes fireflies light up?

Luciferin, a substance in fireflies and other luminescent organisms, produces light when it combines with oxygen in the presence of luciferase, an oxidizing enzyme. The devil really has nothing to do with it.

How do you catch most colds and flus?

Not so much by a sneeze as once commonly thought but by direct or indirect hand contact. If you touch a doorknob, a ketchup bottle, or a fork, for example, that had been previously touched by a sick person, and then touch your own eyes or nose, you may end up intimately acquainted with a total stranger.

What popular American soft drink once contained cocaine?

Coca-Cola. Originally marketed as "French Wine Coca—Ideal Nerve and Tonic Stimulant," the potion also contained wine. When its inventor, pharmacist John Pemberton, took the wine out in the 1880s, then added caffeine and kola nut for flavor, "Coca-Cola" was born.

When did the first diet soda pop hit the market?

In 1952. Cyclamates, a sugar substitute preceding saccharin and Nutrasweet, was used that year in No-Cal Ginger Ale.

What mammal can fly?

The bat.

What tree is pollinated by bats?

The *Adansonia digitata,* or African boabab tree. Its fragrant white flowers open only to the moonlight—just when those pollinating bats are out.

Can you name three mammals that mate for life?

Beaver. Jackal. Some breeds of wolves.

Can you name three birds that mate for life?

Geese. Eagle. Swan.

Can you name three people that mate for life?

What is Lady Ada Lovelace, the daughter of poet Lord Byron, known for in computer circles?

For being the first to arrive at the concept of a computer programming language. ADA, an early military programming language, was named in her honor. A mathematical genius, Ada came up with the idea of punch-card programs to talk to George Babbage's 19-century "difference" or analytic engine, a very rough computer precursor.

Why were the early Church's first great sopranos all men?

Since women were not allowed to perform in church until the early 1800s, "castrati," or castrated men, were used. The castrati were also used in many opera roles in the 17th century and became the world's first superstars, sometimes earning millions of dollars.

What is the longest river in the world?

The Amazon. An explorer named Loren McIntyre is credited with discovering the true source of the river in 1971. Because the headwaters proved to be higher up in the Andes than previously thought, new calculations revised the length of the Amazon River to approximately 4,150 miles, beating the Nile by about 100 miles.

How many rivers feed the Amazon on its way to the Atlantic?

1,100 or so. Seventeen of them are over 1,000 miles long.

How did the Amazon get its name?

Spanish explorers reported seeing fierce, white warrior women on the banks of the river with bows and arrows—not unlike the Amazons described in Greek mythology. Hence, the river's name. Most disregard this story, claiming that since the Spaniards hadn't found the gold they were looking for, they needed a tall tale to tell the king so he would grant them another commission to return and continue their search for "El Dorado" (The Golden One—a place of unimaginable gold and riches).

What is Blue Gum?

Not the latest chew but a popular variety of eucalyptus tree.

How do headhunters make shrunken heads?

After peeling the flesh off of a decapitated head from the neck up and discarding the skull, the eyelids are sewn closed with plant fiber and the mouth is fastened shut with "chonta" spikes. The head is then steeped in water with tannic-rich herbs to shrink it. After 1½–2 hours, the head is removed from the water (now about one-third of its original size) and turned inside out, and all remaining loose tissue is scraped away. Once pared clean, the head is turned right-side out again and hot stones are dropped in through the neck opening. This shrinks

the head still further. The stones are dumped out and the process is repeated with hot sand poured into the nostrils and ears. Later, a hot rock is used to iron the outside of the head, expelling any excess oil and carefully molding it into some hopeful semblance of its onetime owner. Surplus hair is then trimmed away and the head put over a fire to harden and blacken. The "tsantsa," or shrunken head, is now complete except for a tribal ceremony honoring this "trophy" that once sat on the shoulders of an enemy warrior.

What are truffles?

Expensive gourmet mushrooms. A 1997 Christmas Williams-Sonoma Catalogue featured white Alba truffles from Italy for $98 each. NOTE: Large, luscious chocolate bonbons are also called truffles.

Where do you find them?

In wooded areas beneath the ground under oak and hazelnut trees.

How do you find them?

Have a pig or a dog sniff them out. (Pigs, however, are not used much any more since they tend to quickly gobble up the find!)

What do doctors sometimes use to drain the pooling blood in a reattached limb?

Leeches.

Historically, what used to kill more soldiers than bullets?

Disease and infections caused by poor sanitary conditions during wartime. Specifically, typhoid and dysentery killed most soldiers. The outcome of a battle and indeed, even a war, might be determined by the numbers that got sick on one side rather the other side's military prowess.

Who said, "A lie can get halfway around the world before truth has a chance to get its boots on"?

Mark Twain.

Who said, "If music be the food of love, then play on"?

Who else? Shakespeare.

Who was one of the most, if not the most, prolific writer who ever lived?

Spanish playwright and poet Lope de Vega. He wrote over 1,800 three-act plays, most of which were in verse. It was claimed that he could, upon demand, write a play in one day and that he once wrote five plays in two weeks. His output is estimated at more than 21 million verses. He died in 1635 at the age of 63.

What Victorian wit, playwright, and poet went to prison for homosexuality?

Oscar Wilde. It landed him in Reading Gaol (the name of an infamous jail in England) for two years.

Who was the first person to die of radiation poisoning?

Madame Curie, the discoverer of radium.

What famous cowboy stuffed his favorite horse?

Roy Rogers. He taxidermed Trigger and put him on display at his museum in Victorville, California, along with his dog, Bullet, and Dale Evans's horse, Buttermilk.

What very famous writer turned his horse into a duffel bag after it died?

D. H. Lawrence is said to have done this bizarre deed. Presumably, he tanned its hide first.

How do you get the holes in Swiss cheese?

By a gas-emitting bacterium. Other than producing the expanding gases that make the holes, the bacterium also helps flavor and ripen the cheese.

What are a vampire bat's favorite prey?

Unlike Dracula, these creatures of the night prefer pigs, cows, and horses. However, if these can't be found, the vampire bat will feast on humans.

Why does the tiny vampire's bite draw so much blood?

An anticoagulating chemical in the bat's saliva keeps the plasma flowing while he laps it up. Yes, laps. This species of vampire doesn't suck.

What, besides loss of blood, should you worry about if you get bitten by one of these creatures?

Don't worry. You won't turn into a vampire bat, but you could get rabies.

What famous romantic poet is believed to have created the first modern vampire tale?

Lord Byron, aka George Noel Gordon. In the summer of 1816, while at the Villa Diodati in Switzerland, Byron and several friends began telling each other ghost stories one stormy evening. The poet's contribution was published in 1919 from note fragments appropriated by his doctor, John Polidori, who turned them into a story called "The Vampyre." Now considered the first modern vampire tale, it is Polidori, and not Byron, who is credited with writing it. Though "The Vampyre" was originally published in an 1819 magazine that attributed its authorship to Byron, Polidori subsequently claimed that he had really written the story and admitted it was based on the one Byron told that summer in Switzerland. NOTE: The most famous story told at the Villa Diodati that summer, however, was not Byron's but Mary Shelley's: her stormy evening inspiration was *Frankenstein.*

Thalidomide, the fetus-deforming drug taken off the market in the early '60s, is now being used to treat what physically deforming disease?

Leprosy. It is also being considered for the treatment of a variety of autoimmune diseases.

What happens if an octopus damages or loses one of its arms?

It grows a new one. It likes eight.

What is a silverback?

If you guessed a fish or a new punk hairdo, you're wrong. The silverback is the dominant gorilla in a group. It also refers to a mature, male grizzly bear.

What denomination coin first used the phrase "In God We Trust"?

A two-cent coin minted in 1864.

What is the only animal born with horns?

The giraffe. At birth, its horns are flat against its head. Within a week, they pop up.

How many vertebrae do giraffes have in their necks?

Seven. The same as human beings.

To what did Peg Entwhistle, an aspiring actress in the 1930s, owe her dubious celebrity?

In 1932, she committed suicide off the HOLLY-WOOD sign. Some say she jumped from the 13th letter (at the time the sign read HOLLYWOODLAND), as a pitiful, last reference to the bit part she played in her only film, *Thirteen Women*. She, in fact, did nothing quite so creative. She simply hopped off the H.

What is Los Angeles's complete name?

According to a Los Angeles historian, it's El Pueblo de la Reina de los Angeles sobre el Rio de la Porciúncula. Translation: "The town of the Queen of the Angels on the River Porciúncula.*"

* Spanish word meaning "little portion."

What is the "best 'sauce' in the world," according to Cervantes, author of *Don Quixote*?

Hunger.

What language do they speak in Iran (the country formerly known as Persia)?

If you guessed Arabic, you're wrong. It's Farsi.

What is the ancient Japanese practice of seppuku?

Ritual suicide committed by disemboweling oneself with a sword. It is also called hara-kiri or hari-kari. It was mostly practiced by those wishing to avoid execution or disgrace.

What small, furry animal commits suicide?

The lemming. Perhaps to correct overpopulation, lemmings periodically make large migrations to the seacliffs of Scandinavia and hurl themselves to death on the rocks below. Others just scamper into the sea.

Ounce for ounce, what are two of the most expensive animal-hair fibers in the world?

Cashmere (from Tibetan goats) and Vicuna (from a South American camel-like animal of the same name).

What female insect chews her partner's head off during mating?

The preying mantis.

What is the supposed genesis of the "Duck, Cover & Hold" position assumed by children practicing "atomic bomb drills" during the Cold War?

Referred to as the "execution position" during the time of King Henry IV, it was the position assumed by a person who had been condemned to death. Once in that position, large weights (special iron discs of varying sizes) were placed on the condemned's back, which forced the victim's knees into the chest and diaphragm, suffocating him or her to death.

What kind of bird can fly backward?

The hummingbird. Everyone knows it can hover.

How fast can it fly?

Up to 60 mph.

How many times a second does it beat its wings?

50 to 75 times, and even more, say some ento-mologists.

What gourmet delicacy comes from sturgeon, the world's largest freshwater fish?

Caviar. NOTE: Eggs from salmon, cod, lumpfish, etc., are also processed and sold as caviar. In France, however, only the processed roe from sevruga or beluga sturgeon qualify.

What's an erotomaniac?

A person who suffers from the delusion that he or she is loved or desired by another person when, in fact, such a thought may never have even occurred to the other person. Many stalkers are erotomaniacs.

What's a dipsomaniac?

An alcoholic.

What's a trichotillomaniac?

Someone who compulsively pulls out their own hair.

What is trichophobia?

Fear of hair.

What is triskaidekaphobia?

Fear of the number 13.

What is pantophobia?

Fear of fears.

What is the oldest commercial airline in the world?

Avianca, the national airlines of Colombia, established in 1919.

Name one of the very oldest insects on earth—in fact, one of the very oldest *anything*.

Cockroaches. Around for millions and millions of years before we got here, this hearty insect will be skittering about for eons after we're gone.

What, besides the National Organization for Women, is NOW an acronym for?

Negotiable Order of Withdrawal, a term used in banking.

What does the acronym SNAFU mean?

Situation Normal All F***ed Up.

What does the acronym LASER mean?

Light Amplification by Stimulated Emissions of Radiation.

What does the acronym SCUBA mean?

Self-contained underwater breathing apparatus.

What plant is used as both a cure for intestinal worms and as a flavoring for vermouth?

Wormwood. Its blossoms sweeten vermouth and its leaves poison worms.

What is the difference between an alligator and a crocodile?

The overbite. An alligator has a broader snout and its upper teeth overlap its lower ones. Other than the narrower snout, a crocodile has a very large pair of teeth in its lower jaw which fit snugly into the "notches" in its upper jaw. Even when the croc's mouth is closed, this formidable pair of teeth is still visible.

Has the American mainland ever been bombed by enemy aircraft?

Yes. In 1942.

Where?

Near Brookings, a remote town on the Oregon coast.

Who did it?

Japan. Under the cover of darkness, a pilot named Nobuo Fujita dropped two incendiary bombs in a forested area close to the small logging town of Brookings. Three weeks later Fujita repeated the mission in a tiny plane quickly assembled on a Japanese submarine and then shot into the air with a catapult. None of the bombs did much damage but the incidents shook the Western seaboard and put pressure on the U.S. Navy to pull some of their ships out of the Pacific to patrol domestic waters.

What African antelope drinks no water?

The gazelle. The animal "extracts" the moisture it requires from the foods it eats.

Mary Wollstonecraft, author of the radical 18th-century feminist work *A Vindication of the Rights of Women* (first published in 1792), was the mother of what very famous daughter?

Mary Wollstonecraft Shelley, author of *Frankenstein.* Mother and daughter both believed in women's rights and "free love."

What famous poet's body part did *Frankenstein* author Mary Wollstonecraft Shelley keep on her desk after his death?

Percy Bysshe Shelley's heart. Percy was her husband.

What was one of the methods used in the Middle Ages to determine whether or not a woman was a witch?

Trial by water. It was decided that if the accused could float or swim, she was a witch. If the poor thing drowned, her innocence was then confirmed.

Why did NASA begin making the astronauts' space-suits larger after their 1974 stay on Skylab, America's orbiting space station?

NASA doctors reported that all the astronauts on that prolonged mission "grew" taller, one by at least two inches. The reason for this remarkable growth spurt was the environment of "weightlessness" in which they lived. Without the full impact of gravity acting on their bodies, all 23 of the astronauts' intervertebral disks fattened up with moisture and expanded, temporarily stretching out their bodies.

What royal rock star was born an identical twin?

Elvis Aaron Presley. His twin was named Jesse Garren Presley. Jesse died at birth.

What is the most recorded rock 'n' roll song in history?

"Louie, Louie."

Who was the first person to fly over the Andes?

A French woman named Adrienne Bolland did it in 1921. No easy task then, Adrienne had to fly right alongside many of the mountains since her plane couldn't actually get up high enough to fly over them.

What country used women as fighter pilots during World War II?

The Soviet Union. Women were also used as bomber pilots. Marina Chechneva made some 800 combat flights. Another pilot, Natalya Mekin, was credited with almost 1,000 combat missions.

How were American women pilots used in the same war?

Primarily to ferry planes from base to base. A few got to be test pilots. Ann Baumgartner test-piloted the first jet to be used in the Air Force. Other women were employed to tow targets for artillery practice. Twenty-foot pieces of muslin were attached to the wings of their planes and as they flew back and forth, gunnery trainees used the muslin for target practice.

Who killed Cock Robin?

Who cares? But if you do, the sparrow did. In its own words: "I," said the sparrow, "with my bow and arrow."

In what country are the dead given "celestial permission" to return to earth once a year and visit their friends and relatives?

Mexico. During El Día de Los Muertos (The Day of the Dead), or Death Day, cemeteries are turned into picnic grounds. The living bring the dead their favorite foods along with chocolate coffins, sugared skulls, and skeleton toys for the children (living and dead), and have a festive celebration honoring the dead.

What was Elisha Perkins's 18th-century remedy for pain?

What he dubbed the "tractor"—a giant pair of tweezers that Perkins claimed could yank the pain right out of one's body no matter where it was.

What was Brazilian José Arigo's surgical speciality?

Psychic surgery. Operating with a rusty pen knife in the 1950s and '60s, Arigo removed tumors, gallstones, etc., without apparent infection or pain to his patients. Filmed and investigated by countless scientists, doctors, psychologists, and journalists, Arigo was never successfully debunked.

Why was gangster Benjamin Siegel given the nickname Bugsy?

His erratic behavior was thought by some to be "buggy" (in the slang of the time, insane). Hence, the moniker.

What is a "courting stick" and how was it used in the early American colonies?

A long hollowed-out stick, it was used to safely separate a young couple and provide an acceptable means for them to communicate. In the full view of their elders, the "sweethearts" were allowed to whisper to each other through the courting stick.

Whose tooth is venerated at the Tooth Shrine in Sri Lanka?

Buddha's canine.

What is a hemorrhagic virus?

Viruses that can turn human innards to mush and cause bleeding from bodily orifices, eyes and pores included. The eboli virus is an exotic example. A strain of the Hanta virus, transmitted by the common field mouse, is a domestic one.

Did the events portrayed in the film *The Exorcist* really happen?

Yes. Except in real life, it was a boy not a girl who was the object of demonic possession and his head never whirled around like Linda Blair's. That particular incident, as well as the pea-soup projectile vomiting, was Hollywood taking dramatic license. The real events took place beginning in 1949 in Mt. Ranier, Maryland, and went on for several years until "Robbie" was exorcised by a Catholic priest after many, many unsuccessful attempts.

What is rarer than a hen's tooth?

Nothing. Hen don't have teeth.

What masons hewed stones so perfectly that no mortar was required to hold them in place?

The Incas. Not even a knife blade could (or can) be slipped between the stones of their buildings and walls.

Whose nonsaintly remains are on display in a glass-enclosed coffin in a Lima, Peru, church?

Francisco Pizarro, the Spanish conquistador who overthrew the Incan empire with a force of less than 200 men. Disease and superstition, rather than Pizarro's military prowess, however, may be the real reason the Incas were so easily decimated.

What famous English-speaking descendants live on Pitcairn, a small, remote island in the Pacific?

Mutineers from Captain Bligh's HMS Bounty. Led by Fletcher Jones in 1790, a small group of English sailors ended up on Pitcairn with a few Tahitians they picked up on the way and soon began populating their own island.

What very common, ubiquitous bird can live to be 80 years old?

The crow.

What novel is generally considered the earliest Gothic tale of mystery and horror?

The Castle of Otranto by Horace Walpole, published in 1764. *Frankenstein* came 50 years later.

Who is considered to be one of the first, if not the first, commissioned writer in history?

Christine de Pizan (b.1365–d.1431) was commissioned to write the official biography of Charles V of France. Widowed at 25, Christine de Pizan supported her three children off her writing proceeds. Her book, *The Book of the City of Ladies*, is the first feminist work in history.

Who was Beethoven's Immortal Beloved?

No one seems quite sure but a letter hidden in a secret desk drawer found after his death was addressed to her. Whether this letter was a copy of one Beethoven actually sent his Immortal Beloved or just the desperate fantasy of a tortured soul remains a mystery.

What are chopines?

Women's platform shoes worn in the 16th and 17th centuries.

Name one place where the U.S. flag perpetually "flies" at full staff?

The moon.

When the opossum "plays possum," what's really going on?

Contrary to popular belief, the poor critter isn't playing dead. He or she has actually passed out.

What animal species not only mates face-to-face but apparently likes to "do it" for fun as well?

The Bonobo ape of Zaire. It seems these apes use sex for more than just reproduction. They also love to just plain old fool around.

Where do a quarter of all the world's bird species live?

The Amazon Basin.

What wild animal, frequently born in litters of same-sex pairs, is born with fully developed canine teeth and often kills its twin?

The spotted hyena. According to some animal behaviorists, the firstborn will attack and kill its twin whenever possible. Frequently born in litters of same-sex pairs, hyenas may be one of the few wild animals to practice siblicide.

What is the orthopedic designation of Quasimodo's affliction?

Kyphosis, a condition commonly referred to as humpback, or hunchback.

What is the origin of the phrase "a red-letter day"?

It goes back to the Middle Ages, when the Christian calendar designated feast, saint, and holy days in red ink, and all others in black.

Where in the United States do you not have to pay taxes?

On an Indian reservation.

If a group of geese is a gaggle, what is a group of vipers?

A nest.

A group of crows?

A murder.

Of gnats?

A horde.

What itchy skin disease is caused by an arachnid and is highly contagious?

Scabies. Once these mites burrow into your skin and lay their eggs, prepare for torment. Some of their favorite hatching sites are under the breasts, between the thighs, around the waist, and about the genitalia.

Who moves the "planchette," or marker, around on a Ouija board?

Devotees would most likely say "spirits" from another world. A more practical explanation would attribute it to the unconscious muscular movements of the players or participants.

What were three of the many classic films that premiered in 1939?

Gone With the Wind, *The Wizard of Oz*, and *Wuthering Heights*. It was a bumper year for Hollywood with 400 films released. Other classics that year included *Mr. Smith Goes to Washington*, *Stagecoach*, *The Hunchback of Notre Dame*, and *Goodbye, Mr. Chips.* The list goes on.

How did Frank Baum, the author of *The Wizard of Oz*, come up with the "Oz" in his title?

His filing cabinet was supposedly the muse. Divided into A–N and O–Z, a sudden inspiration was said to have been responsible for the latter choice.

What actress turned down the part of Scarlett O'Hara in *Gone With the Wind*?

Bette Davis. She didn't want to play opposite Errol Flynn, who had supposedly been slated for the part of Rhett Butler. The role of Scarlett, as we all know, subsequently went to Vivien Leigh.

What outspoken personality, sometimes actress, and toast of the town during the 1930s, '40s, and '50s said, "I've tried several varieties of sex. The conventional position makes me claustrophobic. And the others either give me a stiff neck or lockjaw"?

Tallulah Bankhead.

Other than from the frozen sperm provided by a sperm bank, can a dead man father a child?

Yes. Using a procedure called "postmortem sperm retrieval," a deceased man's sperm can be used to impregnate a female. Even the sperm of a man who had been dead for 30 hours was successfully retrieved, frozen, and then used to impregnate his widow.

What are the Seven Ancient Wonders of the World?

Colossus at Rhodes, Hanging Gardens of Babylon, Statue of Zeus at Olympia, Temple of Artemis at Ephesus, the pyramid complex at Giza (which includes the Sphinx), Mausoleum at Halicarnassus, Lighthouse of Alexandria.

Which one of the Seven Wonders is still around today?

The pyramid complex at Giza.

What are the oldest living things on earth?

The bristlecone pines in the White Mountains of northern California. Some date back 4,800 years. In other words, the bristlecone pine was around before Moses received the Ten Commandments.

What are the tallest living things on earth?

Redwoods. The Dyerville Giant in Redwoods State Park, California, measured 370 feet when it fell on March 24, 1991. Getting accurate measurements of live trees can be difficult since the tops of them are often hidden by dense branches. The Giant Tree (a live redwood) is somewhere between 257 and 363 feet tall (the height of a 25–26-story building).

Where is the largest living rose tree?

On Toughnut Street in Tombstone, Arizona. Around 9 feet high, its trunk is 13 feet in diameter and its foliage covers 8,000 square feet.

What is the world's oldest written language?

Sumerian. Its cuneiform, or wedge-shaped, inscriptions have been found dating back to 4000 B.C. Sumerian was the language of an ancient non-Semitic people who once lived in the lower valley of the Euphrates.

Why would it be virtually impossible to drown in the Great Salt Lake?

Its high salinity content makes practically everything float.

Where is the highest lake in the world located?

A good guess would be Bolivia's Lake Titicaca at 12,500 feet but the correct answer is an unnamed lake in Tibet.

The male of what marine species has the babies?

The seahorse. The female deposits her eggs into his pouch, where they are fertilized by his sperm. His body then gestates them to term.

After two land snails mate, how come they can both lay eggs?

They're hermaphrodites.

Infibulation, a painful surgical procedure involving the genitals, is primarily performed on whom?

Women, especially those in Africa and India. Except for a small opening left for urination, the labia of a woman's vagina are sewn shut to prevent sexual intercourse. NOTE: Infibulation was used to "cure" male masturbation in several 19th-century European countries. In this case, the foreskin was sewn together with lead wire.

On what grounds did Pope Innocent III (1198–1216) allow the dissolution of marriage?

Genital size. If a couple's privates weren't a good fit, making sex difficult and/or dangerous, the marriage could be dissolved.

What is the world's largest plane?

At present, it's the Russian Antonov, AN-225 Mriya, with a wingspan of 290 feet, a length of 275 feet and 7 inches, and a height of 59 feet and 8 inches. Set one down lengthwise on a football field and it will fall but a mere 10 feet short of the end zones. It wings will extend beyond the width of the field some 63 feet on either side. It's a big bird with a tail section six stories high.

What was one of the largest birds that ever lived?

The elephant bird. Up to 11 feet in height and weighing more than 1,100 pounds, this long-necked oddity had small atrophied wings and massive legs. Exclusive to the island of Madagascar, the elephant bird became extinct in the latter part of the 17th century. A picture of the bird's skeleton in a Paris museum shows a man standing between its legs.

Where is the world's tallest building located?

At present, it's in Kuala Lumpur, the capital of Malaysia. The Petronas Twin Towers, completed in 1997, stretch 88 stories up. If you include their pinnacles, the Towers are much taller, well over a quarter of a mile.

What are the largest fossil remains ever found of an insect?

Those of the dragonfly. With a wingspan of more than 30 inches, this insect was the largest anthropod flitting around several hundred million years ago.

How deep is the deepest part of the ocean?

Over 87,000 feet (16.5 miles) or about the height of three Mt. Everest's stacked on top of each other.

What is the largest nerve in the human body?

The sciatic nerve. Beginning in the low back, this nerve runs down each leg into the feet. Its circumference at some points measures the diameter of your thumb.

What is the human body's largest organ?

The skin, area-wise anyway—14 to 18 feet square feet is the average coverage.

What cartoon is credited as being Walt Disney's first?

Little Red Riding Hood (not *Steamboat Willie* starring Mickey Mouse).

What was the original name of Mickey Mouse going to be before Mrs. Disney nixed it?

Mortimer.

What Celtic warrior-queen is believed to have sacked and burned London to the ground in A.D. 61?

Boudicca or Boadicea (many spelling variations), in revolt against the occupying Romans. Dig down deep enough and in some areas of London you'll find a burnt layer of reddish ash, the supposed physical remains of old "Londinium."

Who was the last person to be locked up in the Tower of London?

Rudolf Hess, the deputy leader of Nazi Germany. Hess was later convicted at Nuremburg and sentenced to life imprisonment at Spandau Prison in Berlin.

How do we know brain surgery was successfully performed many hundreds, even thousands, of years ago?

Holes made in the skull had begun to close, resealing the cranial cavity, proving the patient lived after the operation. There are many examples of "trepanned" (or surgically altered) skulls throughout the world.

What unusual thing occurred the day Alexander Graham Bell filed his telephone patent claim in February 1876?

A man named Elisha Gray filed a patent for a similar invention several hours later.

What notorious, almost legendary, international terrorist has a reputation that is probably more hype than factual?

Carlos the Jackal. According to some accounts, Carlos is mostly myth, a real screwup who botched many of his jobs. In fact, he blew one of his very first assignments when the London businessman he was supposed to assassinate survived a bullet wound to the head. Carlos accidentally shot him in the face. Illich Ramirez Sanchez (the Jackal's real name) is at present in jail.

Why don't mules produce offspring?

They can't. The offspring of a donkey and a horse, mules are almost always sterile.

How long do termites live?

Some queens have reportedly made it to the half-century mark.

What is a book scorpion?

Not a literate arachnid but a variety of creepy crawlies found in old books and papers. They resemble scorpions but have no tails.

What is one of the driest places on earth?

The Atacama Desert in northern Chile. In some areas it has reportedly not rained for hundreds of years. However, the "El Nino" of 1997–98 miraculously moistened up some parts of the Atacama enough to grow flowers. NOTE: An ice-free area of Antarctica known as the Dry Valleys is actually the driest place on earth. It has supposedly been rain-free for a couple million years.

Where do you find the fastest winds on earth?

Inside some tornados.

Where is the windiest place on earth?

Antarctica.

The coldest?

Antarctica.

What kind of wind knocks fruit off trees?

A banana wind. So called in some parts of the Caribbean because it is strong enough to defruit trees but not powerful enough to blow them down.

Relative to its body size what creature has one of the largest penises on earth?

The flea. In its enamoured state, the flea's penis is up to two times the length of its body.

Mariam Rothschild (of the famous billionaire banking family) was an internationally recognized expert in what field of study?

Parasitology, fleas in particular. According to Allan Sherman, a writer, humorist, and crack researcher, Dr. Rothschild supposedly had a very large picture of a flea with an erect penis hanging in her living room.

What famous military genius had an abnormally short penis?

Napoleon. It was said to have been the size of a small finger. Others say it measured little more than an inch. (Atrophy? Could be. He'd been dead for a while.) A rich American urologist purchased the penis in the late '70s for just under four thousand dollars. The rest of the little emperor's body is in Paris.

What famous monk had an abnormally long penis?

Grigori Rasputin. It reportedly measured 13 inches when erect.

What famous gangster's penis was supposedly a freak of nature?

John Dillinger's. For years, rumors circulated that it was 14 inches long when flaccid and 20 when aroused. Rumors that his penis was lost, however, are untrue. It was his brain that got waylaid.

What contemporary American author wrote in a recent novel, "He looks like he's got a cheese danish stuffed in his pants"?

Tom Wolfe, *Bonfire of the Vanities.*

We all know Murphy's Law: "If anything can go wrong, it will." What is Howe's Law?

"Every man has a scheme that will not work."

What film company made not only the first Western but the first horror film as well?

Thomas Edison's own Edison Film Company. It produced *The Great Train Robbery* in 1903 and *Frankenstein* in 1910.

What is the "smelliest" fruit on earth?

The distinction belongs to a tropical fruit called the durian. Some say its odor is so offensive (like sewage or cat puke) that hotels do not permit room service for this disgusting but coveted delicacy. Then, you may ask, why do people eat the durian? Those who've sampled it say it's extraordinarily delicious.

Why do stinkbugs stink?

To keep predators at bay.

Have smells ever been added to a motion picture?

Yes. Switzerland's 1940 film *Mein Traum* (My Dream) was "odorated." The director claimed the audience would be able to smell a variety of wonderful odors including flowers, trees, cooked meat, etc. The new "smellavision" was reportedly achieved by blowing odor essences over the audience with a fan.

Polyester, a 1981 film starring Tab Hunter and directed by John Waters, was released in "Odorama." In this case, the audience was given "scratch-and-sniff" cards keyed to numbers which viewers scratched and then sniffed when those numbers appeared on the screen. The cards contained a veritable bouquet of smells, some not so pretty.

What well-known sisters, all writers, all died of consumption in the middle 1800s scant years apart?

The Bronte sisters—Charlotte, Emily, and Anne (*Jane Eyre*, *Wuthering Heights*, and *The Tenant of Wildfell Hall*, respectively). Anne, Emily, and their brother, Branwell, all died within a year of each other. Charlotte died shortly thereafter.

What absurd thing supposedly happened to the heart of Thomas Hardy (author of *Jude the Obscure* and *Tess of the d'Urbervilles*) upon his death in 1928?

When Hardy died, his heart was removed so it could be interred in Stinsford, his birthplace, and his body laid to rest in Westminster Abbey in London.* Unfortunately, before his heart could be buried, his sister's cat snatched it from a table and made off with it. A tin container, thought by the good folk of Stinsford to hold Hardy's heart, was reportedly buried several days later.

*Another account says his body was originally supposed to have been interred in a nearby town called Dorchester.

What popular spiritual leader said, "You must love those people who irritate you, because they are your gurus"?

The Dalai Lama.

What classic but bawdy book of tales was written during the bubonic plague of the 1300s?

Giovanni Boccaccio's *The Decameron.* The book focuses on the lusty tales shared by a small group of people who flee the plague ravaging Florence and hold up in a villa together. Against this background of fear and despair, seven young men and three women divert each other for 10 days with one story more shocking than the other. After all, what but shock might numb them to the horror around them?

What is the only known life-form with "retractable horns?"

The snail.

What is the offspring of a goat and a sheep called?

A geep. They've reportedly been produced at an animal physiology lab in Cambridge, England, in test tube experiments using surrogate goat and sheep mothers.

What is a geek?

Besides a bright weirdo with few, if any, social skills, the term once referred to a sideshow carney who did outrageous or disgusting things like biting off a live chicken's head.

What heavily populated world capital city is built on a lake?

Mexico City. Tenochtitlán, as the Aztecs called it, actually sits atop several lakes, the largest being Lake Texcoco, in the Valley of Mexico. The lakes have since been filled in, drained, or dried up. As a result, the city is sinking—some say by at least several inches a year.

What household improvement did the Aztecs have that was not yet found in many European cities of that time?

Indoor plumbing.

How many human sacrifices were performed in 1487 for the dedication of Emperor Ahuitzotl's great temple in Tenochtitlán? Hint: It's in the thousands.

In a four-day period, approximately 80,000 victims had their still-beating hearts yanked from their chests and offered to the gods. Some authorities say the figure quoted may be high, but even half that number is daunting.

What were some of the jobs held by the following people before becoming movie stars?

Rock Hudson?

Truck driver.

Sean Connery?

Polished coffins in a woodshop.

Whoopi Goldberg?

Mortuary cosmetologist.

Sylvester Stallone?

Swept out the lion's cages in the Bronx Zoo.

Where did the biggest earthquake in the United States take place?

New Madrid, Missouri, on December 16, 1811. The quake has since been estimated to be a 10 on the Richter scale. Others say it was only an 8+ (whatever that + means). In January and February of 1812, two other giant quakes followed and were said to have caused the Ohio and Mississippi Rivers to flow backwards and ring church bells as far away

as Philadelphia. In fact, this extraordinary earthquake sequence actually changed the course of the
Mississippi River.

What is the Fujita Scale?

A scale developed by Professor Ted Fujita rating
the severity of a tornado based on the damage left
in its wake. The Fujita Tornado Intensity Scale
goes from F1 to F6: F0–F1 = weak; F2–F3 = strong;
F4–F5 = violent. The tornado in Jarrell, Texas, on
June 16, 1997, was an F5 tornado. The twister
ripped an entire subdivision off its foundations.
An F6 tornado would produce such catastrophic
damage that it has been dubbed an "inconceivable
tornado." Winds in such a twister would reach an
estimated 319–379 mph. (Other than for the F6
alluded to in the picture *Turbulence*, such a tornado
has yet to be documented.)

What does the Mohs' scale measure?

The relative hardness of minerals on a scale of
1 to 10. For example, talc rates a 1 and the diamond
a 10.

What is the hardest natural substance in the world?

The diamond.

How many different colors of diamonds are there?

Other than transparent or clear, there are also blue, green, yellow, rose, brown, and orange diamonds. There are even black ones.

What is the largest diamond ever found?

The Cullinan diamond. Discovered in South Africa in 1905, it weighed 3,106 carats. The diamond was eventually cut down to 530 carats and now resides in the British crown jewels.

What popular, contemporary writer of Victorian murder mysteries was once jailed for murder?

Anne Perry. As a young teenager she was an accessory to and/or active participant in the bludgeoning death of her best friend's mother in Christchurch, New Zealand. A condition of Juliet Hulme's (Perry's real name) parole was that she never again see her once-best friend. The 1994 movie, *Heavenly Creatures*, starring Kate Winslet as the young Juliet, recounts the crime.

What popular murder mystery writer is making her way through the alphabet naming her books, letter by letter, starting with *A*?

Sue Grafton. Her first novel was *Alibi. Noose* was her last. *O* through *Z* should be along shortly.

When do you acquire your own unique set of fingerprints?

In the womb. A three-month old fetus is said to already have a distinctive set of prints.

What world-famous billionaire had a pay phone installed in his mansion for guests to use?

J. Paul Getty. Ever the tightwad, Getty supposedly also went through wastebaskets at his home and corporate offices retrieving any paper clips that may have been thrown away, or so it's been said.

Salmonella, a common food poisoning, is a mild form of what deadly disease?

Typhoid fever (salmonella typhosa).

What unfortunate disorder can make a person swear and even grunt or bark uncontrollably in its extreme form?

Tourette's syndrome. The disorder affects men more often than women and is commonly characterized by facial tics and involuntary body movements, such as jerking and twitching.

Other than man, what is the only other creature on earth that makes war (excepting the territorial skirmishes of certain apes)?

Ants. Not only do they wage war, they make slave laborers of the captives they don't kill.

How many times its own body weight can an ant lift?

Twenty. (Some sources say up to 50 times its own weight.)

After the queen ant mates, how long can she continue to lay eggs from that one mating?

Between 15 and 17 years in some species, as long as she lives.

What is a formicary?

An anthill or ants' nest.

What modern monarch lists his occupation as "employee of the state" and drives a Harley-Davidson?

King Juan Carlos I of Spain.

What percentage of the human body is made up of water?

Seventy percent.

What waxy, grayish substance thrown up from the sperm whale's intestines was once used in the manufacture of some perfumes?

Ambergris. The substance caused scent to cling to the skin longer. It has since been replaced by synthetic applications.

What is a shooting star?

A meteor or "meteorite." Upon entering the earth's atmosphere, it appears as a bright, streaking flash as it burns up.

At what speed does a tsunami, or tidal wave, travel?

At the speed of a jet plane, or about 500 miles per hour. A tsunami is caused by an underwater earthquake.

What does pumpernickel mean in German?

Devil's fart. It was said that when the bread was first invented, it was so bad it could make even the devil fart from gas and indigestion.

Where may Bram Stoker, the Irish author of *Dracula*, have gotten his idea for killing vampires with a stake?

In Ireland during the last part of the 1800s, people who committed suicide had a stake driven through their hearts and then were buried in unconsecrated ground.

Within $10 million, guess the highest amount ever paid for a painting?

$82.5 million. That's how much a Japanese paper tycoon paid for Van Gogh's *Portrait of Dr. Gachet* in 1990.

What well-known poster boy for cigars has supposedly not smoked one in over 10 years?

Fidel Castro.

What is the sex of a singing canary?

Male. Females can't sing.

What is meant by the expression, "When you hear hoofbeats, think horses not zebras"?

The more logical explanation is usually the correct one.

What are two mammals that have the smallest birth sizes relative to their adult size of any mammals on earth?

The panda. When it is born, the panda is smaller than a mouse. The kangaroo is even more diminutive. At birth it is not much bigger than your fingertip.

What fish, a popular delicacy in Japan, can cause toxic shock, respiratory failure, and even death, if improperly prepared?

The puffer fish. It can be 270 times more toxic than cyanide. But properly prepared, "fugu" (a sushi favorite) causes a slight high and tingling sensation throughout the body.

What is one of the most expensive, if not the most expensive, spice in the world?

Saffron. It takes an acre of crocus plants to produce just 10 pounds of the spice.

What language has more words than any other language in the world?

English.

The world has approximately how many different languages?

Five thousand, depending how you count.

What bird's eyes are bigger than its brain?

The ostrich.

How old was the world's oldest pig when it died?

Over 65. Breed or sex unknown.

Who was history's biggest polygamist?

King Solomon. The foxy old patriarch liked to seal political alliances with marriage and picked up 700 wives and 300 concubines along the way. Some sultans and tribal chieftains may claim more wives but they are not as well known as Solomon.

What Egyptian pharaoh has a condom named after him?

Ramses. Ramses II fathered over 100 kids.

What Egyptian Queen had no Egyptian blood in her?

Cleopatra VII (the one we all know). She was Macedonian Greek.

How did the ancient Egyptians count the number of enemy dead after battle?

By tallying up severed body parts, usually in the form of a hand, tongue, or phallus. The soldiers did the cutting. The scribes did the counting.

How did the ancient Egyptians believe humankind was created?

On a potter's wheel fashioned by Khnum, the Egyptian ram-headed, creator god, using the mud of the Nile.

Why do most Egyptians drive without their car lights on at night?

The Egyptians say it's because they don't want to "wear down their batteries" and/or because "it's rude to shine your lights at oncoming traffic." Apparently, most of the headlights you see in Cairo belong to foreigners.

What popular mystery writer is a fully accredited Egyptologist?

Barbara Michaels aka Elizabeth Peters aka Barbara Mertz. Under the first two aliases she has written many fictional works including *The Mystery of the Black Tower* and *The Crocodile on the Sand*, respectively. She reserved her real name, Barbara Mertz, for scholarly books on Egypt such as *Red Land, Black Land: Daily Life in Ancient Egypt* and *Temples, Tombs, Hieroglyphs: A Popular History of Ancient Egypt*.

Why are there dolphins, sharks, stingrays, and other oceanic fish in the Amazon River?

The Amazon Basin used to be a vast inland sea open to the Pacific rather than to the Atlantic. However, when the Andes heaved upward some two to four million years ago, this sea was cut off from the Pacific, trapping many saltwater species. In time, a flow of water toward the Atlantic created the Amazon River with many former oceanic fish now adapting to a freshwater existence. Including the long-snouted dolphin, shark, and stingray, there are over 50 oceanic species in the Amazon.

What's the name of that "thing" hanging down at the back of your throat?

Uvula. It vibrates when you pronounce certain sounds.

What do you call that notch in your upper lip?

Philtrum.

What's that hollow at the bottom of your neck known as?

Suprasternal notch. Or, if you're inclined to be romantic, the Almasy Bosphorus as claimed and named by Count Almasy (the Ralph Fiennes role in *The English Patient*) for that alluring spot on his lover's neck.

What thin band of tissue keeps you from swallowing your tongue?

The frenum.

What's the diving speed of a Peregrine falcon?

Speeds well in excess of 200 miles an hour.

What is the world's largest rodent?

The Capybara. An Amazon water hog that looks like a big guinea pig, it can weigh more than 100 pounds.

What is one of most poisonous and perhaps the fastest snake on earth?

The black mamba. Known for its stealth and aggression, this African snake will sometimes stalk its victims and, when on the attack, move in spurts up to 15 miles an hour.

What is a "hairy star"?

A comet (Latin derivation).

Where is the world's fourth largest pyramid?

Las Vegas. The Luxor (a casino).

What was one of the original meanings of *casino*?

A public room, or place, for social gatherings, dancing, and music. Its association with gambling came later.

Is there any difference between innervate and enervate?

Yes. The former means to stimulate and the latter, to weaken or debilitate.

When are *regardless* and *irregardless* interchangeable?

Never. *Irregardless* is not a word but a crime against the English language.

What famous American naturalist observed, "Any fool can kill a tree. They can't run away"?

John Muir.

What English playwright and critic gave the advice, "If you can't hide the skeleton, make it dance"?

George Bernard Shaw.

What well-known English romantic poet was also a doctor?

John Keats. Unfortunately, he couldn't help himself. He died of tuberculosis at 26.

What famous explorer, given to bouts of severe depression, killed himself after he and his partner returned from their history-making expedition out West in the early 1800s?

Meriwether Lewis of Lewis and Clark. He shot himself. He considered the expedition a failure.

What insect dies the same day it is born?

The mayfly. It departs 18 hours later.

What insect species is toxic to birds because it fed on a poisonous plant (milkweed) while in its larval form?

The monarch butterfly. If a bird should be unwise enough to nibble on one, it will instantly throw the monarch up.

Are all rattlesnake bites harmful?

No. Up to 40 percent of rattlesnake strikes are purportedly "dry bites" and contain little or no venom.

When a man and woman walk down the street, why does the man customarily walk on the outside, closest to the curb?

The custom goes back to the days preceding indoor plumbing in Europe and England when chamber pots were emptied out of second-story windows into the gutters below. Later, it prevented horses and buggies, then cars, from splashing mud and water, or whatever, on milady.

What is the "China Syndrome"?

An uncontrolled nuclear reactor meltdown. In such an instance, the failure of emergency systems and reactor coolant loss causes the reactor core to overheat, become molten, and burn its way through the floor toward China (so to speak). It came close to happening at Three Mile Island, Pennyslvania, in 1979 and at Chernobyl in 1986.

Where did O. Henry, the celebrated short-story writer, supposedly get his name?

In jail. While serving three years for bank fraud, William Sidney Porter adopted the name of his prison guard, Orrin Henry, as his own and shortened it to O. Henry.

What is piffle?

Nonsense.

What's the origin of the "private eye" logo?

The Pinkerton Detective Agency. Founded in the 1800s, the agency's wide-open eye symbolized its motto, "We never sleep."

What well-known, spy-thriller author was himself a spy and former Eton master?

John le Carré, author of *The Spy Who Came in From the Cold* (1963).

What is the most popular recurring character in the history of movies?

The role of Dracula. In one form or another it's been done at least 130 times.

Who is usually credited with writing the first detective story?

Edgar Allan Poe. His character, Chevalier C. Auguste Dupin, first made his appearance in Poe's story, "The Murders in the Rue Morgue" (1841).

What was the murder weapon in Roald Dahl's short story, "Lamb to the Slaughter"?

A frozen leg of lamb. The evidence was then cooked by the woman who whacked her husband into oblivion and fed to the officers investigating the crime for dinner.

Sir Arthur Conan Doyle, the creator of Sherlock Holmes, practiced what profession unsuccessfully before becoming a mystery writer?

Medicine.

What well-known healer spent most of the last 50 years of her life in bed suffering from an undiagnosed illness?

Florence Nightingale.

***Little Caesar*, written by W. R. Burnett in 1929, is considered the first example of what kind of popular fiction?**

The gangster novel.

What detective was supposedly the first to utter "Crime does not pay"?

Dick Tracy.

Why is Broadway called "The Great White Way"?

Because of all the lights.

What was the first thermometer filled with instead of mercury?

Brandy. Dating back to at least the 1600s, this spirited predecessor of today's thermometers was quite accurate.

The Bible is the object of what frequent criminal activity?

Theft. It is reportedly one of the most, if not the most, stolen book in America.

How did Leah win back Jacob's affections in the Book of Genesis and get him to sleep with her again?

With an aphrodisiac called mandrake. Leah's success resulted in Jacob's fifth son. The plant, vaguely resembling a human being, was believed to be a love potion in Biblical times and is still used in some parts of the world today for that same purpose.

What ancient civilization thought rotting fish entrails were an exquisite aphrodisiac?

The Romans.

Who said, "Power is the ultimate aphrodisiac"?

Henry Kissinger.

What is the smallest independent nation in the world?

The Holy See, or the Vatican. Occupying approximately 108 acres in the middle of Rome, the Vatican has its own army, newspaper, and post office.

When did the pope become infallible?

In 1870. It was then that Pope Pius IX, the 253rd successor of St. Peter, declared himself infallible on matters of faith and morals.

Do women have souls? After debating the question at the Council of Macon in A.D. 585, guess what early Church prelates decided?

The good fathers decided by one vote that, yes, women were human. They had souls. NOTE: Today Church theologians dispute this interpretation of the debate and its outcome, saying the whole thing was a ridiculous misunderstanding—a matter of semantics, not dogma.

Which Holy Father was accused of turning the papal palace into a whorehouse?

The dubious honor goes to the "unholy" 10th-century pope, John XII. His unquenchable sex drive produced as much animosity toward the papacy as it did mistresses for his bed. Poetic justice was served when horny John was thrashed into eternity after being caught in "flagrante delicto" by the husband whose wife he was delicto-ing.

Why was the missionary position once the only acceptable method of sexual intercourse recognized by the Church?

All positions other than "man on top" were considered unnatural. Early theologians thought anything else reversed the natural order of things and/or interfered with conception.

What revered saint and icon of the Catholic Church said, "Prostitution is a necessary condition of morality" and "If you put down prostitution, license and pleasure will corrupt society"?

St. Augustine.

Who is the patron saint of lovers?

St. Valentine.

What important position did Joan Anglicus once occupy in the Catholic Church?

Some claim she was its pope from A.D. 853 to 855. The Church, of course, denies this but one prominent Vatican librarian has recorded her stint in the papacy as fact. To make a long story short, Joan passed for John. But when Pope John got pregnant, the jig was up.

What former man made her professional tennis debut as a woman in the mid-'70s?

An ophthalmologist named Dr. Richard Raskind. In his female incarnation, he became Renee Richards and caused quite a stir on the courts. After an attempt to bar her from playing, Renee filed a lawsuit and won based on the fact there was ample physical evidence to prove "she" was now all female.

What jazz pianist and saxophonist from the 1940s to the 1960s was really a woman passing herself off as a man?

Billy Tipton. Married three times, not even Tipton's adopted sons realized he was a woman until he died. He supposedly used the "old war injury" excuse to avoid conventional sex with his wives.

Before electricity came along, how was "limelight" created?

By heating blocks of lime until they glowed. Beginning in the 1850s, these incandescent blocks were used as stage illuminators.

What is dry ice?

Carbon dioxide solidified into cakes of ice. The fogging or misting occurs as it vaporizes. It never passes through a liquid state.

What was the last planet to be discovered in our solar system that has not yet been explored by any kind of space probe?

Pluto*. Discovered in 1930, it is usually the outermost planet (its orbit is elliptical) in our solar system. Within the next decade, a NASA mission now dubbed "Ice and Fire" will send an exploratory space vehicle to Pluto. It will arrive at its destination 12 years later.

*A dozen or so new planets have recently been discovered. Termed extra-solar, these planets do not orbit our sun but other stars in our solar system.

If a cameo is a figure raised on stone, what is its reverse called?

Intaglio. In this case, the figure is engraved below the surface of the stone.

What languages appear on the Rosetta stone?

Greek, ancient Egyptian demotic, and hieroglyphs. Discovered in 1799 by Napoleon's troops at Rosetta, Egypt, it gave linguists and archaeologists the key they needed to decipher the language of the ancient Egyptians.

Where is the Blarney Stone?

Ireland. In Blarney Castle in the village of Blarney.

Why do people kiss it?

So they can acquire a gift for blarney or the knack of smooth, persuasive talk.

What is the correct way to kiss the Blarney Stone?

You lean backwards until your lips touch the Blarney Stone which is located between the castle wall and the parapet. It's probably a good idea to grab on to the iron bars provided or have someone hold you by the ankles while you attempt this very acrobatic maneuver. If not, the Blarney Stone might be the last thing you kiss.

What film had one of the longest precredit sequences (action occurring before the title and credits) in movie history?

The Last Movie. Made by Dennis Hopper in 1971, the film rolled on for a good half-hour before the title of it or the name of the actors in it ever appeared on screen.

What sexy actress, popular in the 1950s and early '60s, said, "Hollywood is a place where they'll pay you a thousand dollars for a kiss and fifty cents for your soul"?

Marilyn Monroe.

How many different variations of barbed wire are there?

At least four hundred and probably more since that's how many patents were filed in the latter half of the 19th century. Collectors will pay thousands of dollars for some of the rarer varieties.

When was DNA "fingerprinting" first introduced as a technique for solving crimes?

In 1987. In January of the following year, a man in England who had been charged with rape and murder was convicted on DNA evidence.

What is the origin of the Internet?

It was created by the Department of Defense in 1969 as a decentralized communications system in the event of nuclear attack. Also designed to coordinate military research projects, ARPAnet (Advanced Research Projects Agency network) quickly grew to include various universities doing defense-related studies. The idea was for "the network" to share research data.

What American president had a marijuana patch in his backyard?

George Washington. At the time, the hemp fiber was used for ropes. If he ever smoked it, he never inhaled. Would George lie?

What president served the shortest term of anyone elected to that office?

William Henry Harrison, the ninth president. He died 31 days after his two-hour inauguration from a cold he caught that day which turned into pneumonia.

What president had electricity installed in the White House and then was afraid to use it?

President Benjamin Harrison (1889–1893). The president and the first lady were so afraid of being mortally zapped after the execution of ax murderer

William Kemmler in the electric chair on August 6, 1890, they rarely turned the lights off in the White House, even in the bedroom. After all, if the flick of a switch could fry Kemmler, why not the president or his wife? It took a while for many people to get used to Edison's new invention. In the beginning it inspired as much fear in some people as it did awe.

Who was the youngest first lady ever?

Frances Cleveland. She was just 21 when she became the first lady. Up until that time, Frances was Grover's ward, having been orphaned at 11.

Who was an executioner before becoming president of the United States?

Grover Cleveland. He personally hung two convicted criminals.

What U.S. president may have held that office under false pretenses?

Chester A. Arthur (1881–1885). Some sources believe he was born in Canada. Under the Constitution, only people born in the United States are eligible to be president.

Who was the only president never to marry?

James Buchanan (1857–1861). A lifelong bachelor, rumors at the time linked him with "Miss Nancy," William Rufus Devane King, the vice president in the administration preceding his.

What president probably died of medical malpractice rather than an assassin's bullet?

John Garfield (1881). Seven months after taking office, Garfield was shot by Charles Guiteau. At his trial, Guiteau admitted to shooting the president but not to killing him. He said the doctors did that. Most experts agree. An autopsy of the president showed all the poking and prodding by his doctors in search for the bullet not only damaged Garfield's innards but caused most of the hemorrhaging and infection that ultimately killed him. Guiteau was executed anyway.

Has the United States ever been without an acting president?

When James Polk's term expired on Saturday, March 3, 1849, Zachary Taylor refused to be sworn in on the Sabbath, or Sunday, opting instead for Monday, March 5. According the the law of succession at the time, the president pro tempore of the Senate, or David Rice Atchison, would have served as the acting president on Sunday. However, it appears Atchison was never "officially" sworn in. So, either the nation was without a president on Sunday, March 4, 1849, or David Rice Atchison was president for a day.

What president's father told him, "If you were a girl, you'd be in the family way all the time. You can't say no"?

Warren G. Harding.

What American founding father wrote a pornographic essay entitled "On Choosing a Mistress"?

Benjamin Franklin. Congress later spent thousands of taxpayer's dollars reportedly trying to buy up all the copies.

What bird did Benjamin Franklin want as our national symbol instead of the eagle?

The turkey. He proposed it to the Continental Congress in 1789.

What African capital is named after an American president?

The Liberian capital, Monrovia, is named after James Monroe, fifth president of the United States (1817–1825).

When was the first U.S. television broadcast?

1927. Herbert Hoover, secretary of commerce at the time, had his image broadcast from Washington, D.C., to New York.

What does the word *football* refer to in conjunction with the president of the United States?

A very special briefcase handcuffed to the wrist of a military officer who follows the president around. The "football" contains each day's new missile launch codes so that no matter where the commander-in-chief is, he can order a full-out nuclear attack. Rumors once had Ollie North quarterbacking the "football."

What is a suitcase bomb?

A portable, one-kiloton Russian nuclear bomb whose outside container resembles a suitcase. One person can detonate it and kill tens of thousands of people in a heavily populated area.

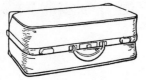

What is "pulp fiction"?

Other than the name of a 1994 film, it is a term referring to the cheap pulpy paper on which detective magazines ("pulps") were published in the 1920s and '30s.

When was the first opera performed?

1597. *Daphne*, written by Jacopo Peri, was first staged in Florence that year.

Who was opera's first superstar "diva"?

Baldassare Ferri, a castrato. Upon his death in 1680, the very successful Ferri left today's equivalent of $3 million to charity.

In opera, what is meant by a "trouser role"?

Roles where women wear the pants. It is actually a man's role written to be sung by a woman, such as the part of Octavian in Strauss's *Der Rosenkavalier*.

In what city did the Phantom of the Opera live?

Paris.

What tin-earred millionairess, great aficionado and lover of opera, once rented Carnegie Hall so she could sing her favorite arias?

Florence Foster Jenkins, on October 25, 1944. By now in her 70s, charming, screechingly awful Florence made her debut. Did this Diva know how bad she really was? If she did, she chose to ignore it and the critics as well. It seems Florence's voice was so ghastly that only morbid fascination can explain why so many people remained rooted to their seats listening to her.

Is the Tasmanian Devil a real, live animal or just the nickname of a once-popular actress?

Both. It is a flesh-eating marsupial native to Tasmania and the moniker of Merle Oberon, a once-popular actress who was also Tasmanian.

Who invented champagne?

An 18th-century monk named Dom Perignon. When he replaced his wine bottles' leather and wooden stoppers with cork ones, the good Dom discovered the secret of sealing the bubbles inside. Hence, the birth of champagne. His first sip of bubbly inspired the immortal line, "I am drinking the stars."

Who invented the margarita?

An American woman named Margarita Sames claims she did in 1948. Her recipe: a good tequila (such as Jose Cuervo or Blue Agave), Cointreau, ice, and fresh lime juice. No Triple Sec. (Salt is optional.) Anything else, she says, is simply not a margarita!

Who invented the cotton gin?

Some think a Southern belle named Catherine Littlefield Greene did. According to some accounts, the usually credited American inventor Eli Whitney got the actual plans for the invention from her. Others say no, that she only gave him the idea for the cotton gin and financed its development. In either case, she got no credit.

Who invented paper?

A Chinese eunuch named Ts'ai Lun around A.D. 105. The invention made him rich and impressed the Emperor so much he gave Ts'ai Lun a title. Before the invention of paper, the world relied on parchment, and before that, on papyrus, both of which were scarce and difficult to prepare.

Who invented the brown paper bag?

Marjorie "Mattie" Knight patented her machine for making paper bags in 1870.

What popular office product, once called "Mistake Out," made its inventor a millionaire?

A poor typist, Bette Nesmith Graham, took to using white paint to cover up her mistakes rather than lose her job. Hence, out of sheer necessity, "Liquid Paper" was born. Bette improved on the white wall paint she originally used before patenting her own timesaving magic formula.

Who "invented" Nutrasweet?

A drug company. A serendipitous discovery made by Searle Labs is responsible for giving the world aspartame ("Nutrasweet"), an amino acid derivative several hundred times sweeter than sugar. Among other ingredients, Nutrasweet contains methanol. Yes, methanol, a substance known to be poisonous in even small amounts. However, the FDA and all interested parties aver and swear that the amount contained in Nutrasweet is not a noteworthy toxicological concern. It would be interesting to know what the researchers at Searle were really looking for when they stumbled across Nutrasweet.

What is a micropantograph?

Invented in the early 1920s, the machine was developed to send secrets during wartime. Its extraordinary technology allowed for the inscription of over four thousand words on a surface no larger than a grain of rice.

What country gave eunuchs the right to vote in 1994?

India.

What happens when you hit your "funny bone"?

You stun, or aggravate, your ulnar nerve (the one that passes through a notch in your elbow and runs the length of your arm), which produces that "funny" don't-know-whether-to-laugh-or-cry sensation radiating out from your elbow.

What blind insect has been described as a killing machine, destroying everything in its path?

The driver or army ant.

What was the "Make-Believe Ballroom"?

An imaginary ballroom where the Depression's poorest radio listeners could go in their heads every week and enjoy themselves. Premiering on KNEW-AM in 1934, the radio show played the day's best dance music and let its audience's imagination create a magical night out on the town.

What marine mammal did some early explorers mistake for mermaids?

The manatee. Hard to believe since there's hardly the barest resemblance. Some of the confusion may derive from sailors witnessing the manatee's very humanlike behavior of cradling their young with their flippers and suckling it at their breast.

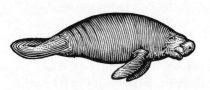

What characteristic do marine species living at the bottom of the ocean share with fireflies?

They glow in the dark.

What is the largest office building in the world?

The Pentagon. It has 6.5 million square feet.

What ex-Marine (who allegedly wore red panties and a bra under his uniform) achieved notoriety in the 1940s and '50s directing hilariously awful B movies (mostly horror) and dressing in women's clothes?

Edward D. Wood, Jr. All who knew him are quick to clarify that he was not a homosexual but a transvestite, or cross-dresser, who just couldn't help putting on women's clothing. It made him feel wonderful. His girlfriend, however, didn't share his enthusiasm. When she found out the lingerie he bought wasn't for her, the relationship was over.

From what is Howard Hughes's plane, the Spruce Goose, constructed?

Mostly wood, mostly spruce. Built during World War II, "non-strategic materials" had to be used. At the time, the "flying boat" was largest aircraft ever built with a wingspan 100 feet longer than that of a 747. Designed to serve as a hospital in air, the Spruce Goose flew only once and for only about a minute. By the time Hughes completed it, the war was over.

What wood was Noah's ark traditionally said to be made of?

Gopher wood. The etymology of "gopher wood" supposedly means laminated wood. The lamination, in this case, was achieved by gluing together layers of planking with tree sap resin. Those who believe they have located the ark say the deck planking shows evidence of lamination.

How high can insects fly?

Some species can flit comfortably along at altitudes between 2,000 and 4,000 feet.

What is the etymology, or word origin, of "testify"?

Testes. According to one lawyerly source, the fellows in the Roman court used to swear on their testicles.

Betties, Goolies, Slappers, and Love Spuds are all slang words referring to what?

The Family Jewels, the testicles.

What's a dowcet? Hint: Not to be confused with a docent.

A deer testicle. Considered a delicacy in medieval England.

What's a flibbertigibbet? Hint: Not an insect.

A flighty person.

What's a capon? Hint: Not an hors d'oeuvre.

A castrated rooster.

Why is the cashew technically not considered a nut?

It doesn't have a shell. It grows as a seed and is found, not on trees, but on shrubs.

Was there ever such a thing as a flea circus?

So they say. Among other things, these Lilliputian performers were supposedly "trained" to dance and play "flea music" and wear teeny-weeny costumes. However, sources on this subject are mute as to how any of this was actually accomplished.

What common vegetable brought to the Old World from the New were the English initially afraid to eat?

The tomato. They thought it was poisonous.

What oil from a common plant seed makes a deadly poison?

The castor-bean plant. Its oil contains ricin, a highly toxic protein that agglutinates red blood corpuscles. Isolated as a white powder, ricin is said to be up to 100 times more toxic than the venom of some cobras.

What country's economy was once totally dependent on bird droppings?

Naurú. This small island country in the Central Pacific once had one of the highest per capita incomes in the world based on "guano," a phosphate-rich birdshit. During the 19th century, Peru also did very well selling guano. Europe bought much of it to fertilize their fields.

What is the only food that never spoils?

Honey.

What is a "Chatham" emerald?

An emerald that has been "grown" in a laboratory. Its molecular structure closely resembles that of a real one. In some cases, only a gemologist can tell the fake emeralds from the real thing. Rubies, sapphires, and other gemstones can also be produced in the laboratory. The process takes 8 to 12 months. At least six companies, including Chatham, presently produce commercially created gemstones.

What Greek philosopher thought love was "a grave mental disease"?

Plato.

Who believed diamonds were made from the fires of love?

The Italians. That's probably why diamonds were used in medieval times for engagement rings. Made from the hardest of elements, the Italians believed diamonds were destined to last forever—just like true love.

What is a coral reef made of?

The porous, limestone skeletons of tiny animals.

What is the largest, living creature on earth?

The blue whale. One specimen measured 110 feet, the height of an 11-story building.

How much of an iceberg is actually under water?

Ninety percent.

What's the world's smallest monkey?

The pygmy marmoset. An inhabitant of the Amazon rain forest, this tiny guy weighs in at only 3 to 4 ounces when fully grown and measures but a mere 6 inches.

Who was the world's largest suit of armor made for?

An Indian elephant. The armor is now in the Tower of London.

Injections of what deadly poison are now being used to get rid of facial wrinkles?

Botulinus, a bacterium so lethal that one teaspoonful of it could wipe out an entire city. A minute amount of diluted botulinus called Botox (a synthesized botulinus toxin) makes crow's feet and brow furrow lines disappear—at least for a while. Treatments have to be repeated about every six months.

How much water can a 10-gallon hat hold?

Less than a gallon.

Why is the candirú açu, a minute, almost invisible catfish in the Amazon River, so greatly feared?

It can force its way up the human uretha and cause physiological havoc. Once the little bugger fans out its thorny spines, it is almost impossible to extract short of surgical intervention. Ouch!

How far away is the farthest galaxy in the universe (to date anyway)?

Eons. An estimated 13 billion light-years away.

How accurate is the atomic clock at the U.S. Naval Research Laboratory in Washington, D.C.?

To within 1 second every 1.7 million years. That's why time-sensitive businesses and the military set their clocks to it.

Is it conceivable that tens of thousands of people could all disappear in the same sandstorm without leaving a trace?

That's what supposedly happened in 525 B.C. in the Sahara Desert. A fierce sandstorm suddenly blew up and King Cambyses II of Persia lost an entire army beneath the dunes near what is today the Egyptian–Libyan border. Expeditions to date have failed to produce physical proof of such a tragedy but those who believe it really occurred say it's only a matter of time before the desert once again reveals what it now conceals.

Where do Central and South American natives get the deadly poison they dip their darts in?

From a frog. The dendrobatid species is commonly referred to as the poison dart frog.

What animal has striped skin beneath its fur?

The tiger.

What insect has two brains?

The cockroach. One in the head and a lesser one in its tail.

Just how dirty are cockroaches?

As dirty, or clean, as their surroundings. They constantly groom themselves.

What phenomenon purportedly accounts for a hefty percentage of all global warming?

Insect flatulence. Sound like a joke? Not if you're concerned about the greenhouse effect. Such is said to produce as much as 20 percent of all methane gas emissions. If not the cockroaches and other crawlies, then perhaps the fault lies with domesticated animals. It has been claimed that sheep, cows, and other animals that ferment their food (and fart a lot, of course) produce incalculable amounts of methane, a major greenhouse gas. It sounds like the roaches and the cows are being set up to be the fall guys for the sins of the industrial world.

Where was the earliest known toilet seat found?

In the city of Akhetatem, Egypt (from circa 1350 B.C.). Seats made of stone, pottery, and wood were used on top of large bowls of sand.

What mammal's heart beats only nine times a minute?

The whale.

How was an "attempted suicide" punished in 19th-century England?

By hanging whomever made the failed attempt.

Approximately how many different varieties of apples are there?

Around 8,000. Included in this number, however, are wild apples and ones that are not necessarily edible.

Any idea how long it would take to make over a million dollars a day if your starting salary of $1 were doubled each consecutive day? Note: On this job you have to work weekends.

Less than a month. On the 22nd day to be exact. At that time your salary would be $1,937,032.

What about a billion?

A little over a month. On the 32nd day. Your salary would then be a mere $1,983,520,768.

How does the "Horny Toad" (it is actually not a toad at all but a lizard) defend itself against predators?

Among other things, it squirts a stream of blood at them from the corners of its eyes.

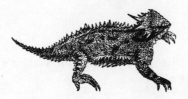

What is an ecdysiast? Hint: It's a fancy word for someone who may or may not bare their soul as well.

A stripteaser.

What animal has black skin beneath its fur?

The polar bear. The gorilla also has black skin.

Was there ever a month that didn't have a full moon?

Yes. February 1865 is reportedly the only month sans a full moon in recorded history.

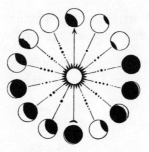

What insect's bite may cause the victim's skin to gangrene or rot off?

The brown recluse's. Also called the violin spider because of markings resembling a fiddle on its back, the recluse's bite is extremely poisonous and potentially lethal. Antibiotics are used to combat the bite's toxic effects and to help prevent the skin from rotting and sloughing off around the puncture site.

What unusual thing happened to Phineas Gage at a Cavendish, Vermont, railroad yard in 1848 which should have killed him instantly?

An explosion drove a three-and-a-half-foot iron rod measuring one-and-a-quarter inches in diameter and weighing over 10 pounds through his cheek, up through the front of his brain and out the top of his head. The iron rod landed some 30 yards away. According to accounts of the accident, Phineas remained conscious afterward and was even able to walk around and talk coherently. Except for a blinded eye, he was pronounced physically cured of his wound several months later. His personality, however, took a sharp turn. Phineas wasn't so agreeable anymore.

What play was Abraham Lincoln watching when he was assassinated?

A comedy called *My American Cousin* by Tom Taylor.

Where does the expression "Your name is mud" come from?

From Dr. Samuel A. Mudd, the doctor who treated Lincoln's assassin, John Wilkes Booth. Mudd doctored the broken ankle Booth got jumping onto the stage after he shot Lincoln at the Ford Theater. As a result, Mudd was reviled and the expression "Your name is mud" came into being. NOTE: Mudd and Booth had met previously, perhaps as many as three times. Mudd was sentenced to life in prison as a coconspirator.

What is the most common name in the world?

Mohammed.

Who was the first author to present a typewritten manuscript for publication?

Mark Twain. It was his novel *Life on The Mississippi* and not *Tom Sawyer* that was submitted to a publisher in typescript. (Twain historians are the ones who decided which novel it was. Twain thought it was Tom Sawyer.) NOTE: Although Twain fooled around on the typewriter, someone else typed his handwritten manuscript of *Life on the Mississippi* before it was sent off for publication.

How often do "intersex" births, or births with "ambiguous genitalia" (a combination of male and female anatomical structures), occur?

More often than you might think. Statistics say that one in every 20,000 births (some say even less) is an intersex baby with some degree of "ambiguous genitalia." Intersexuality, or hermaphroditism, is a complicated and misunderstood syndrome that is becoming increasingly controversial because of the way the medical community has dealt with this condition. For decades, doctors decided which sex the baby should be and operated to remove any structures that didn't define their choice for the child. In many instances, the results proved devastating as these children matured into adulthood. It seems the psychological consequences of arbitrarily deciding a person's sex after birth are very complex indeed. Gender selection (if any), say intersex individuals, should be their choice exclusively.

What does the largest active salt mine in the world have besides lots of salt?

A cathedral that seats thousands of people. Located deep in a mountain outside Bogota, Colombia, the impressive Catedral de Zapaquirá is carved completely out of salt with arched ceilings seven stories high.

What kind of behavior is exemplified by a dog that licks your face while pissing on your leg?

Passive-aggressive.

Who opined, "Maybe this world is another planet's hell"?

Aldous Huxley.

What is "Frankenfood?"

If you guessed that it's something Dr. Frankenstein might have cooked up, some experts would agree. "Frankenfoods" are gene-altered, or "genetically engineered," food. Besides gene-spliced milk (bovine growth hormone added), there's now pork with human genes, potatoes with waxmoth genes, cornbread with firefly genes, etc. Lettuce, melons, wheat, coffee, and apples are just a few of the other foods on a very long list that are being tampered with genetically. At present the FDA does not require any labeling on most "Frankenfoods." Scary? Tsk. Tsk. How can you be afraid of a monster you can't see?

What is the omnipresent "&" symbol called?

Ampersand.

What famous Los Angeles landmark flashes out "Hollywood" in Morse code?

The Capitol Records building. Built to resemble a stack of records, a red airplane-warning light atop the structure flashes out the name of Tinseltown every 20 seconds or so.

What did they used to grow in Beverly Hills before it became Snootsville, USA?

Lima beans. In addition to farming, sheep were also raised there in the 1880s. But just try and get the present residents to admit any of this.

What deadly fish killer inhabits several rivers in the eastern United States?

Pfiesteria piscicida. This microscopic killer shoots a paralyzing toxin at its prey and then promptly proceeds to eat holes in its flesh. Fast and efficient, Pfiesteria piscicida's victims are soon belly-up.

What sainted French woman reportedly still looks the same as she did the day she died in 1879?

St. Bernadette. On view in a glass-enclosed coffin in a French chapel, people claim her flesh never corrupted and that she is as beautiful as ever.

What Egyptian pharaoh's mummy is still entombed in the Valley of the Kings where he was first discovered?

Tutankhamen, or King Tut. It is only Tutankhamen's sarcophagus that people have seen on display around the world.

What happened to King Tut's penis after his tomb was opened?

It disappeared. Whether it was misplaced or stolen is unclear.

The Paris Catacombs are home to how many dead occupants?

One estimate is 6 million. A true "City of The Dead," as it is often called.

Which daughter of Isabel and Ferdinand of Spain carted her dead husband's body around for months before burying him, constantly opening his coffin to make sure he was still there?

Juana La Loca (Joanna the Crazy). Insanely jealous of her husband's flirtations in life, Juana remained so in his death, convinced some woman might still want to steal him away from her.

What famous 14th-century Italian poet did everyone briefly believe dead only to see him live another 30 years?

Petrarch (of sonnet fame). Laid out for mourners to view his body, the poet supposedly sat up after almost a day of being dead and complained of a chill in the room. Is it true or was Petrarch the ultimate prankster?

What famous composer's head was separated from his body for 145 years?

Franz Joseph Haydn's. Several days after Haydn was buried in 1809, amateur phrenologist and prison warden Johann Peters secretly dug the composer up and cut off his head. He then quickly reburied the body and made off with Haydn's noggin. After divesting the skull of its flesh, Peters confirmed what he had suspected all along—the composer's head had fully developed music bumps—supposed phrenological proof of his genius. The jailer then gave the skull to Josef Rosenbaum, the onetime secretary of Haydn's former patron, Prince Esterhazy. Rosenbaum's wife fashioned a display case for the cherished relic and proudly exhibited it for all their guests. After an ensuing odyssey through many curious hands, the itinerant skull was at last reunited with its body in 1954 and the esteemed composer was finally reburied in one piece.

What happened to Eva Peron's embalmed body after her widower, Juan Peron, was ousted from the Argentine presidency in a 1955 coup?

The generals responsible for the coup had Eva's body moved from place to place over the next 16 years. It was even buried for a while in an unmarked grave in Milan, Italy. In the early 1970s, Eva's body was exhumed and finally returned to Argentina.

Where did a blind 16-year-old French boy named Louis Braille get the idea that would enable the sightless to read and write?

From a French military officer who invented a system of night communication. Since lighting a match to read a message might prove fatal on the battlefield, Captain Charles Barbier devised a grid of raised dots that his men could use to talk to each other. Twelve dots in all, they were grouped and regrouped into various combinations to stand for letters and sounds. Louis Braille modified Barbier's 12 dots to 6 and developed the Braille method used by the blind today.

Where in the body do you find a complete sample of your DNA?

Your hair. Its root bulb yields a complete DNA blueprint.

What legendary rock star was really a blond who dyed his hair black?

Elvis Presley.

Who wrote his offbeat, "All-American" novel in less than three weeks?

Jack Kerouac. The first draft of his *On the Road* best-seller was supposedly completed in just 20 days, an average daily output of 8,750 words.

By how many votes did President Andrew Johnson (1865–1869) escape impeachment?

One. Charged by the House of Representatives with high crimes and misdemeanors (among other things, for attempting to throw Edwin Stanton, his secretary of war, out of office), Andrew Johnson was tried by the U.S. Senate in 1868 and spared the ultimate disgrace of impeachment by a single vote.

Who is "Andy Gump?"

A man whose name has become synonymous with portable privies. Founder of a multimillion-dollar corportion by the same name, Andy Gump has the unique distinction of being immortalized by those nomadic toilets used by millions at special events and construction sites throughout America.

What famous gangster once broke out of jail with a wooden gun?

John Dillinger. In 1934 he escaped from an Indiana jail by jamming a wooden gun into a guard's stomach as the door to his cell was opened. "Under gunpoint," Dillinger forced the guard to take him to the warden's office where he traded in the wooden gun for a few real weapons. After locking up several dozen guards and miscellaneous personnel, Dillinger stole the sheriff's car and drove across the border.

What were "Fat Man" and "Little Boy" benign nicknames for?

The atomic bombs dropped on Nagasaki and Hiroshima, respectively.

Where is the greatest amount of gold supposedly on deposit?

In a Manhattan Federal Reserve vault, and not at Fort Knox.

How many different words are there for snow and ice in the Eskimo or Inuit language?

Hundreds.

Did George Washington really wear false teeth?

Yes. But they weren't wooden ones as generally believed. They were fashioned from animal teeth. Elephants, sheep, deer, and various other animals all contributed to George's dentures.

Drop for drop, what insect's venom is the most toxic?

The black widow's.

Where is the tallest or highest waterfall in the world?

Venezuela. Spectacular "Angel Falls" drops some 1,000 meters or approximately 3,300 feet. That's more than twice the height of the Empire State Building.

Who said that "The surest sign that intelligent life exists elsewhere in the universe is that it has never tried to contact us"?

Sam Watterson, *Calvin and Hobbes.*

ABOUT THE AUTHOR

Tanya Slover is a published author, poet, and screenwriter. She has ghostwritten extensively for doctors, and has a background in anthropology.